COLLECTIONS

A Harcourt Reading / Language Arts Program

*The welcome mat
is out. Come in,
come in!*

COLLECTIONS

A Harcourt Reading / Language Arts Program

WELCOME HOME

SENIOR AUTHORS

Roger C. Farr • Dorothy S. Strickland • Isabel L. Beck

AUTHORS

Richard F. Abrahamson • Alma Flor Ada • Bernice E. Cullinan • Margaret McKeown • Nancy Roser
Patricia Smith • Judy Wallis • Junko Yokota • Hallie Kay Yopp

SENIOR CONSULTANT

Asa G. Hilliard III

CONSULTANTS

Karen S. Kutiper • David A. Monti • Angelina Olivares

Harcourt

Orlando   Boston   Dallas   Chicago   San Diego

Visit *The Learning Site!*

www.harcourtschool.com

ISBN 0-15-312041-X

2 3 4 5 6 7 8 9 10   048   2001 2000 99

WELCOME

HOME

Dear Reader,

    Welcome Home is a book about all those who are special to us — our families, pets, friends, and neighbors. You will read stories about families and neighbors who help each other. You will learn how to find your own place on a map. You will even meet some friends of the future! We hope you will share these stories with someone you would like to welcome home.

                Sincerely,

                The Authors

                The Authors

theme

Hello, Neighbor

4

Contents

Hello, Neighbor

Reader's Choice

ASK MR. BEAR
By Marjorie Flack

Ask Mr. Bear

by Marjorie Flack

What makes a good gift for mother
on her birthday? Mr. Bear knows!

ALA Notable Book
FROM THE LIBRARY

8

Leon and Bob
by Simon James

What will Leon and his
make-believe friend Bob do
when a new boy moves
next door?

FROM THE LIBRARY

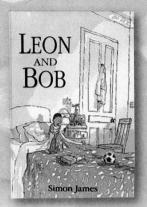

Fire Fighters
by Norma Simon
Illustrated by Pam Paparone

Firefighters are busy
helping their community
fight fires and keep safe.

FROM THE LIBRARY

9

A Bed Full of Cats

Award-Winning
Author/Illustrator

by Holly Keller

Flora is Lee's cat. She is as soft as silk. Flora
sleeps on Lee's bed. Lee likes it that way.

When Lee moves his feet under the quilt, Flora jumps on them. **Thump!** When Lee wiggles his fingers under the sheet, Flora tries to catch them. **Swish!**

When Lee pets her, Flora purrs. **Purrrrrr . . .**
When Lee sleeps, Flora sleeps, too.

One night Lee had a bad dream. He wanted Flora. She wasn't on his quilt.

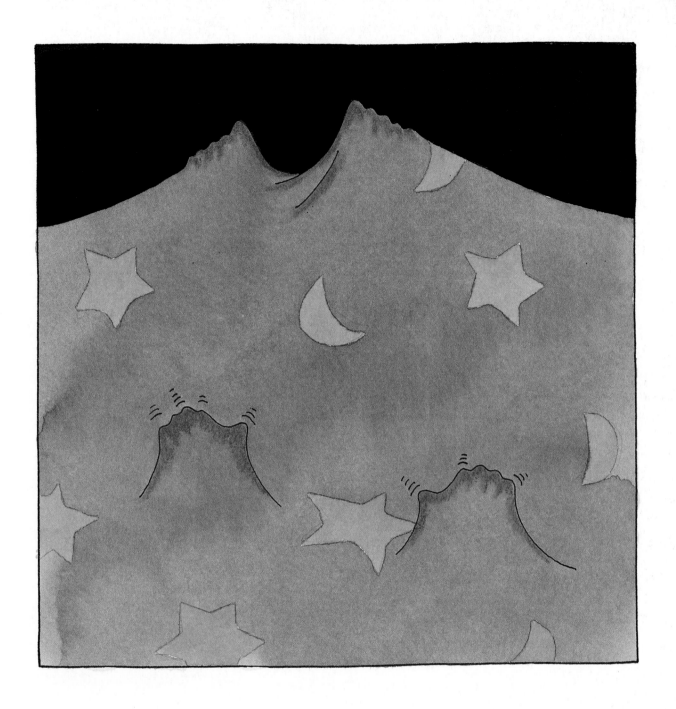

He moved his feet, but Flora didn't jump
on them. He wiggled his fingers, but Flora
didn't try to catch them. He wanted to
hear her purr, but Flora was not there.

15

The next day Flora was not in Lee's room.
She was not on Lee's bed. Lee didn't know
where Flora was.

"You should try to look for her," said Mama.
"We'll help you," Papa said.
"She'll come home when she needs to eat,"
said Grandma.

Lee looked for Flora in the house.

Mama looked all around the garden.

Papa looked in the trash bins.

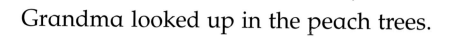

Grandma looked up in the peach trees.

Flora didn't come home. Lee was very sad.
His eyes were full of tears. If only Flora
would come back! "Please come home,"
Lee cried.

"We could put an ad in the newspaper,"
Papa said. "What should we write?"
"Write this," said Lee. "We lost our cat,
Flora. If you find her, please call. Then give
our number."

Lee didn't hear anything about Flora.
No one found Flora, and she didn't
come home. Days and weeks went by.

Then one night Lee felt something on his bed. He moved his feet under the quilt. **Thump! Thump, thump, thump, thump!**

He wiggled his fingers under the sheet.
Swish! Swish, swish, swish, swish!
Lee sat up and turned on his lamp.

There was Flora—with four kittens!
"Flora is home!" Lee yelled. "And that's
not all!"
Mama, Papa, and Grandma ran to
Lee's room.

Now Lee has a bed full of cats and he likes it that way. Those cats are as soft as silk. They are also fun.

**Thump, thump.
Swish, swish.
Purrrrrr!**

Think About It

1 Where did you think Flora was as you read the story?

2 What would you have done if you were Lee and your pet was gone?

3 What did the author do to make the end of the story a surprise?

25

Visit *The Learning Site!*
www.harcourtschool.com

Meet the Author/Illustrator

Holly Keller

Some of Holly Keller's ideas for this story came from things that her children did. When her children, Corey and Jesse, were little, they wouldn't sleep without their favorite stuffed animals on their beds. Corey's favorite stuffed animal was a mother cat with kittens, just like Flora in the story.

Teacher Read-Aloud

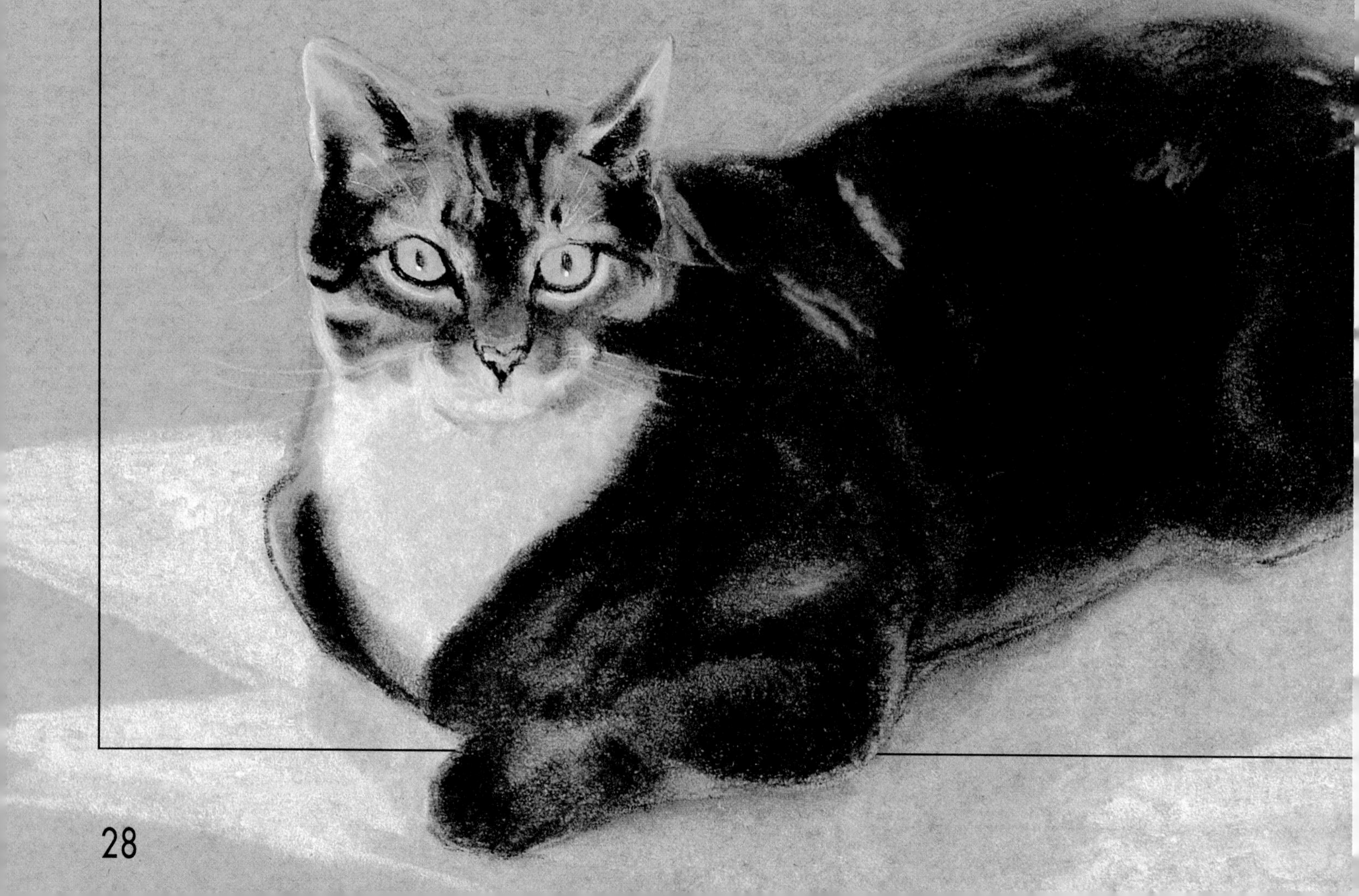

Our Cat

The cat goes out
    And the cat comes back
And no one can follow
    Upon her track.
She knows where she's going,
    She knows where she's been,
And all we can do
    Is to let her in.

by Marchette Chute
illustrated by Ed Young

Response ★ Activity

A Book Full of Pets

**In the story, Lee loves his cat.
What is your favorite kind of pet?**

YOU WILL NEED:

▲ paper ▲ crayons or markers
▲ tape ▲ pencil ▲ stapler

Think about your favorite kind of pet.

Draw a picture of the animal.

Write the things you like about the animal. Tell why you would like to have that kind of pet.

I like fish.
They swim.
They are pretty
to watch.

I love dogs.
They play with you and
they are good friends.
My dog licks my
face all the time.

When everyone is done, put your pages together to make a class book.

Think about how to order the pages. Make a cover and staple all the pages together.

Our Class
Book
of Pets

THE MAP

by Joan Sweeney

Illustrated by
Annette Cable

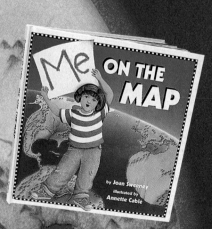

This is me.
This is me in my room.

This is a map of my room.

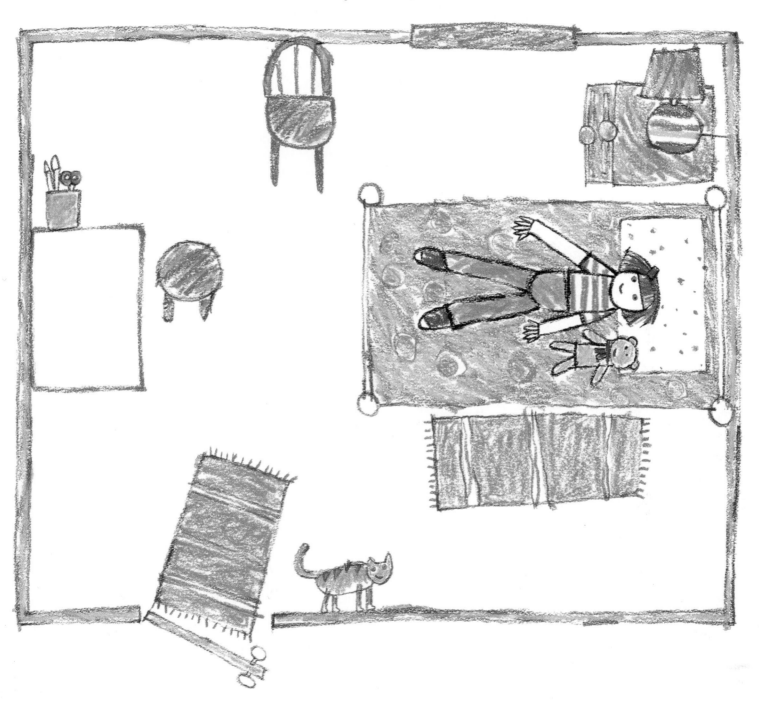

This is me on the map of my room.

This is my house.

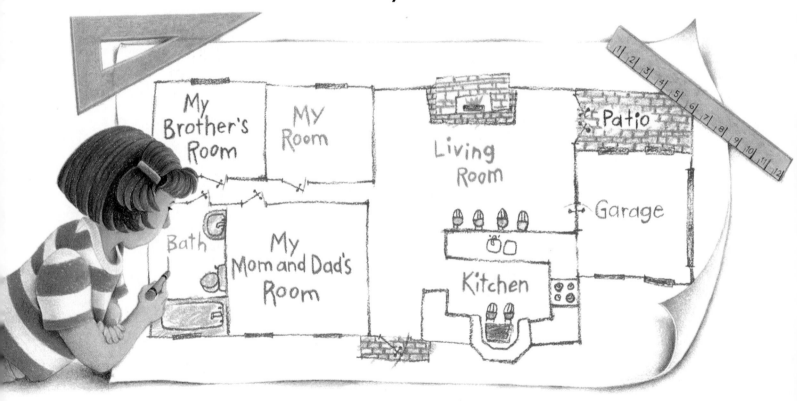

This is a map of my house.
This is my room on the map of my house.

This is my street.

This is a map of my street.
This is my house on the map of my street.

This is my town.

This is a map of my town.

This is my street on the map of my town.

This is my state.

This is a map of my state.

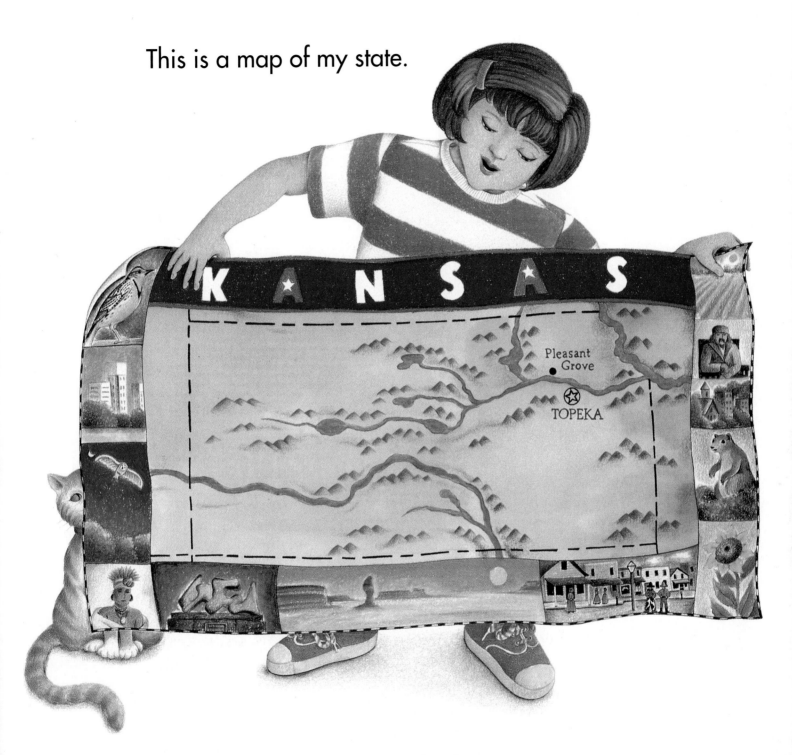

This is my town on the map of my state.

This is my country. The United States of America.

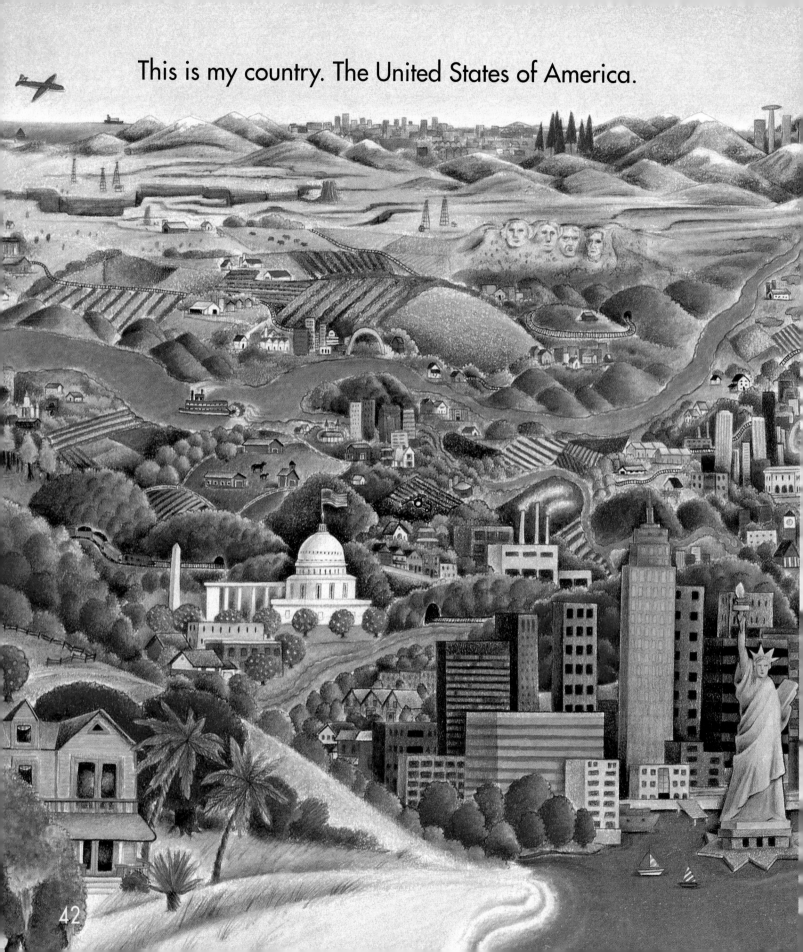

This is a map of my country.

This is my state on the map
of my country.

This is my world. It is called Earth.
It looks like a giant ball.
If you could unroll the world and make it flat . . .

. . . . it would look something like this map of the world.

OUR WORLD

NORTH
AMERICA

EUROPE

ASIA

AFRICA

SOUTH
AMERICA

AUSTRALIA

ANTARCTICA

This is my country on the map of the world.

So here's how I find my special place on the map. First I look at the map of the world and find my country.

OUR WORLD

NORTH AMERICA

SOUTH AMERICA

EUROPE

ASIA

ANT

AUSTRALIA

Then I look at the map of my country and find my state.
Then I look at the map of my state and find my town.

Then I look at the map of my town and find my street.

And on my street I find my house.

48

And in my house I find my room.
And in my room I find me!
Just think . . .

. . . in rooms, in houses, on streets,
in towns, in countries all over the world,
everybody has their own
special place on the map.

51

Just like me.
Just like me on the map.

Think About It

1 How has this story changed the way you think about where you live?

2 What did you learn from reading the story?

3 How do the words and pictures work together to give information?

Meet the Author and Illustrator

Joan Sweeney

Joan Sweeney wrote *Me On the Map* to help children learn about maps. She has written three other books in this series, one about how the body works, one about space, and one about families.

 Visit *The Learning Site!*
www.harcourtschool.com

Annette Cable

When Annette Cable was your age, she let people know what she was thinking by drawing pictures. She used real maps to help her draw the ones in *Me On the Map*. She wanted the maps to be just right, so she spent a lot of time drawing them.

Joan Sweeney

Annette R. Cable

53

RESPONSE ACTIVITY

YOU ON A MAP!

Draw a map of a place that you know well.

YOU MIGHT CHOOSE:

- your house or your room
- your favorite park
- a place you like to shop
- your classroom
- the playground

If you can, go to the place. Look carefully at the main objects in the place. Notice where each object is. Draw your map. You may want to draw it in pencil first and then color it.

Share your map with classmates. Tell about why you chose that place.

Lilly's Busy Day

written by Julie Verne

illustrated by Betsy Everitt

Lilly Feeny was a happy baby—
most of the time.

One day, Mr. and Mrs. Feeny had
to go out.

Katie came to baby-sit Lilly.

"Lilly," said Mrs. Feeny. "Katie will be playing with you today."

"Hello, Lilly," said Katie. "Let's have fun!"

"Funny fun in the sunny sun," sang happy Lilly.

"Good-by, Lilly," said Mr. Feeny as he left.
"Good-by, Lilly," said Mrs. Feeny as she left.
Happy Lilly left, too. In her place was
crabby Lilly. She started to yell.

"I want my mommy!" yelled Lilly. "I want my daddy!"

"Stop it, Lilly!" cried Katie. "Be nice!" Lilly just cried harder.

"What can I do?" thought Katie.

"Lilly, are you hungry?" Katie asked. "Would
you like something to eat?"
"I want jelly," said Lilly.

61

Katie fixed a jelly sandwich. She watched Lilly eat until she was full. Lilly was happy. She was just a little sticky.

"Let me clean you up," said Katie. All too soon, crabby Lilly was back.

"I want Mommy and Daddy!" she said.

"OK, Lilly," Katie said. "Let's go outside."

"I know," said Katie.
"We can go to the park."
"Barky bark in the park," sang Lilly.

64

"Why didn't I think of this before?" thought Katie. In no time at all, they were at the park. Katie and Lilly played on the swings and in the sandbox.

Then they went to feed the ducks. "Look at that funny duck, Lilly!" Katie said. "All the other ducks are just swimming." Lilly started to laugh.

After the ducks swam away, the girls moved
on. They saw some puppies in the grass.
Lilly played with the puppies.
"Now she's silly Lilly," Katie thought.

67

They saw some men at the ball field.
"Daddy? Where's Daddy?" Lilly cried. "Where is Mommy?"
"Not again!" groaned Katie. "Here comes the other Lilly."
"I want Mommy! I want Daddy!" cried Lilly.

"Let's go, Lilly," said Katie.
"I want Mommy, Katie!" yelled Lilly.
"I want Daddy, too!"
Lilly cried until she fell asleep.

Soon they were back at Lilly's house. Katie had to carry sleepy Lilly into the house. "In one day, Lilly was happy, crabby, sticky, silly, and sleepy!" she thought. "What a busy day for little Lilly!"

Lilly opened her eyes just as Mr. and Mrs. Feeny walked in.

"Hello, Lilly," said Mr. Feeny.
"Do you want us to play with you?"
"No," said Lilly. "I want Katie!"

Katie just had to laugh.

Think About It

1 Who do you think had a harder day, Katie or Lilly? Why do you think so?

2 Have you ever spent time with someone like Lilly? Tell about what happened.

3 What did you learn about Lilly and Katie?

71

Meet the Illustrator

Betsy Everitt

Betsy Everitt thought about her own two children when she illustrated "Lilly's Busy Day." She liked reading about how Katie tries to understand Lilly and finds ways to make her happy. When she isn't illustrating, Betsy thinks of fun things to do with her children.

Visit *The Learning Site!* www.harcourtschool.com

72

73

RESPONSE ✿ ACTIVITY

Poems About Feelings

Everyone has feelings. You can write a poem about feelings.

What makes you feel, happy, sad, silly, angry, or afraid? Decide what to write about. You may want to write about:

- one feeling or many feelings
- a special day
- a special person
- the most fun you ever had
- a time when you were surprised or scared

Write your poem.

When you finish, copy the poem onto a sheet of paper. Draw pictures for your poem.

Then share your poem with a group.

Award-Winning
Author/Illustrators

SPLASH!

by
Ariane Dewey and Jose Aruego

"**W**ake up, you big fur ball!" Nelly yelled.
She gave Sam a shake. "Why do we always
sleep late?"

"Don't be a pest, Nelly," Sam growled. He turned his back on her.
"Just once," said Nelly, "I'd like to be on time. Are you awake?"
"No, I'm dreaming," Sam said.
"Well, dream about fat, floppy fish," Nelly said.

She rushed out of their cave. Sam jumped up
and ran after her.

"Is that sound a splash?" asked Sam.
"I bet it's bears," said Nelly. "Let's hurry, before all the fish are gone."

Together, they ran to the river.

"I hate to be late!" said Nelly.
The river was full of bears catching fish.
"Oh, no," the bears groaned. "Here come
Sam and Nelly!"

"It was nice while it lasted!" said one bear.
"What kind of mess will they make this time?"

Nelly slipped on a wet rock. She fell into the river. Splash!

"I'll save you!" Sam yelled, slipping after her. Splash again!

Together, Nelly and Sam made a wave
that tipped over ten bears.

"What's the matter with you two? This isn't a game," growled one bear.
"Sorry! We made a mistake," cried Sam.
"We are sorry!" Nelly added. "Please don't chase us away."

"OK, OK. You can fish with us," said the other bears. "But for once, behave."

"Don't forget, we bring good luck," Nelly bragged. "The biggest fish don't get here until we do."

While she was talking, their lunch swam by.
The bears had never seen so many fish in one
place. All they could hear was the sound of
swishing fins.

"Quick! Get them before they're gone!" Sam yelled. Hungry bears snapped at the fish. The river was a jumble of fins and fur.

Brave fish swam to a deep lake.

91

In the end, most of the fish were safe. All of the bears were full. Sam and Nelly walked home to their cave.

"We wake up late," said Sam.

"And we are clumsy," said Nelly, "but we do have fun!"

Now all they needed was a
good long nap!

Think About It

1. Do you like Sam and Nelly? Tell why
or why not.

2. How do the other bears feel about
Nelly and Sam? How do you know?

3. What did the author/illustrators
do to make the story funny?

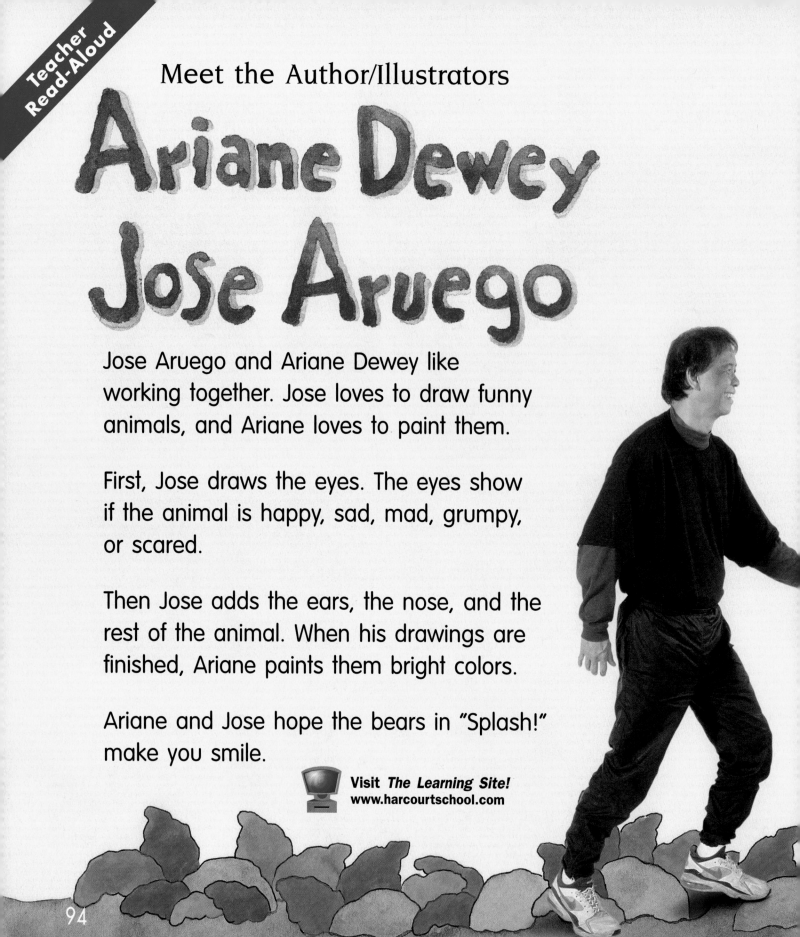

Meet the Author/Illustrators

Ariane Dewey Jose Aruego

Jose Aruego and Ariane Dewey like working together. Jose loves to draw funny animals, and Ariane loves to paint them.

First, Jose draws the eyes. The eyes show if the animal is happy, sad, mad, grumpy, or scared.

Then Jose adds the ears, the nose, and the rest of the animal. When his drawings are finished, Ariane paints them bright colors.

Ariane and Jose hope the bears in "Splash!" make you smile.

Visit *The Learning Site!*
www.harcourtschool.com

Lift-the-Flap Science Book

What do animals eat? Make a book that shows what one animal eats.

First, choose an animal. Find out what that animal eats. Follow these steps to make a lift-the-flap book.

Bear Food

What do bears eat?

1 Fold your paper. Write a title.

2 Open the paper. Write a question about what your animal eats.

3 Draw an outline of the animal's body.

4 Now draw the food the animal eats in its stomach. Color.

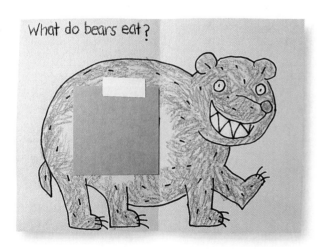

5 Cut a piece of paper to cover the food. Tape it over the food in your animal's stomach.

6 On the back, write a sentence that tells what the animal eats.

Put your book in the class library.

My Robot

Award-Winning Author

by Eve Bunting
illustrated by Dagmar Fehlau

I got a new robot for my birthday. I call
him Cecil. Ever since I got him, we have
been doing lots of things together.

99

Cecil plays tag with the children at school.
WHIR! WHIR! We hear the sound of his
wheels spinning as he races after us.
Sometimes he goes a little too fast.

CRASH! SMASH!
Cecil hits the fence.
"Not the fence, Cecil!" I call. It's hard not
to laugh. Playing tag is not the best thing
my robot can do.

All my friends at school like Cecil a lot. He helps our teacher, Mr. Spencer. Helping Mr. Spencer is not the best thing my robot can do.

Cecil leads the school band.
RUM-A-TUM-TUM. Hear that drum.
"Don't dance, Cecil!" I say. "Don't
prance! Just march!"
The children in the band march along
after him. Leading the band is not the
best thing my robot can do.

Cecil picks me up after school.
He gives me a ride home.
"How's the weather up there?"
my little brother Dennis asks.
He gets a ride home, too.

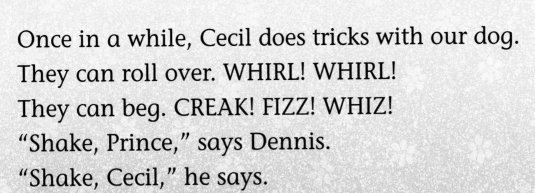

Once in a while, Cecil does tricks with our dog.
They can roll over. WHIRL! WHIRL!
They can beg. CREAK! FIZZ! WHIZ!
"Shake, Prince," says Dennis.
"Shake, Cecil," he says.
Doing tricks is not the best thing my robot
can do.

Cecil plays hide-and-seek, too. He is always IT. He gives everyone a chance to find a good place to hide.

CLANK! CLUNK! Here comes Cecil!
We don't say we heard him coming. He
whistles when he finds us. WHIR! SPARK!
POP! Playing hide-and-seek is not the best
thing my robot can do.

Everyone has heard about Cecil's cakes.
He makes circus animals with the frosting.
His cakes are almost too pretty to eat.
"This is your best cake yet!" says Dennis.

"Cecil's cakes are pretty good," I say, "but that is still not the best thing my robot can do."

"My tummy tells me it is," Dennis says.

Cecil can mow the grass.
WHIR! WHEEZE! WHISH!
Cecil goes very fast. It's a hot
day, but Dad is not hot.

"This <u>must</u> be the best thing Cecil can
do," says Dad.
"Almost," I tell Dad. "You and Dennis
come with me. I'll show you something
else Cecil can do."

111

"Look in here. Even cleaning my room is not the best thing my robot can do." I give Cecil a hug.

"Thanks, Cecil," I whisper. "The very best thing you can do is be my friend!"

FLASH! SPARK! WHIRL! POP!
Cecil knows.

Think About It

1 If you had a robot, what would you want your robot to do for you?

2 What does Cecil do for the boy in the story?

3 What do the pictures tell you about when this story takes place?

Meet the Author
Eve Bunting

Dear Boys and Girls,

I once met a robot. Students had made him out of cardboard. He was a great robot! Each of the boys and girls took him home for one night.

I thought about how grand it would be to have my very own robot. So I wrote a story about one and called it "My Robot." I am happy to share it with you.

Eve Bunting

Meet the Illustrator

Dagmar Fehlau

Dear Boys and Girls,

I was born in Germany, and then I came to the U.S. to study art. I always loved drawing and painting, so I knew I would be an artist when I grew up. When I finished school, I began to do illustration work. I hope you like the pictures in "My Robot."

Dagmar Fehlau

Visit *The Learning Site!*
www.harcourtschool.com

115

Visit the Robot Zoo

The Body Works Issue

chickaDEE

Discover a World of Fun

$2.95

Jan./Feb. 1998

Get in the Swim with a visit to the Robot Zoo

PLUS

Slalom Thrills and Spills, **and more!**

stroke!

Polar bear

Want to find out how animal bodies work? Then visit the Robot Zoo. You'll see machines built to copy animals, using nature's own designs. Looking at these robots can help you to understand how real animals work!

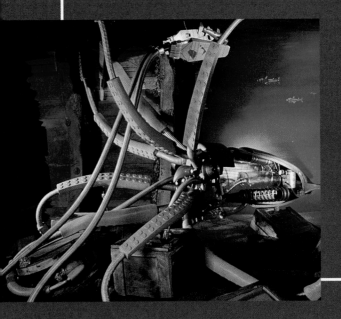

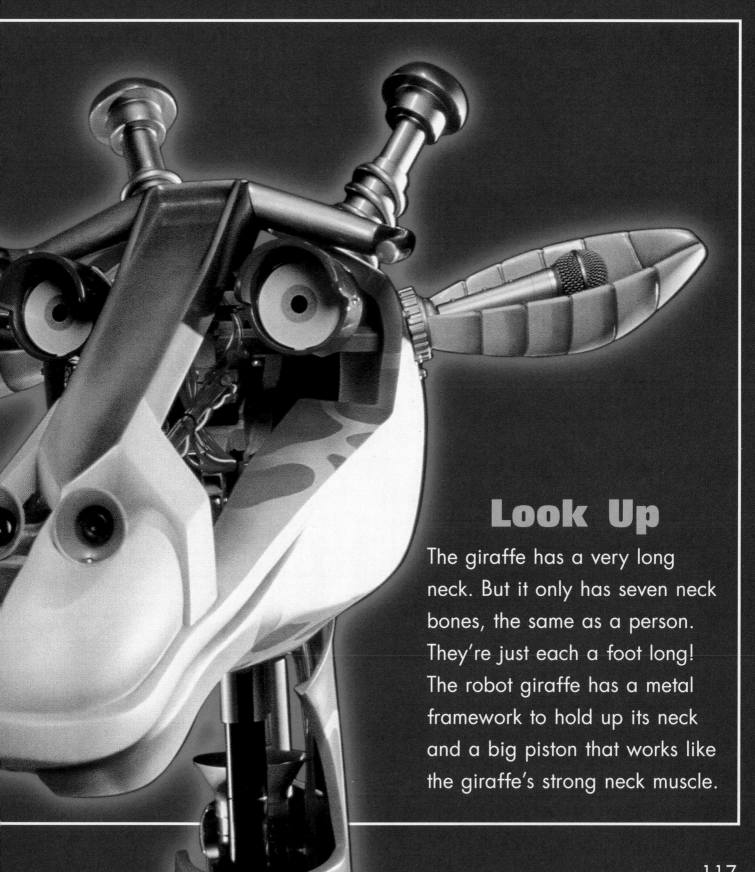

Look Up

The giraffe has a very long neck. But it only has seven neck bones, the same as a person. They're just each a foot long! The robot giraffe has a metal framework to hold up its neck and a big piston that works like the giraffe's strong neck muscle.

Buzz Off

A house fly is so hard to swat
because both of its eyes have
about 4,000 six-sided lenses.
They help the fly see just
about everything!

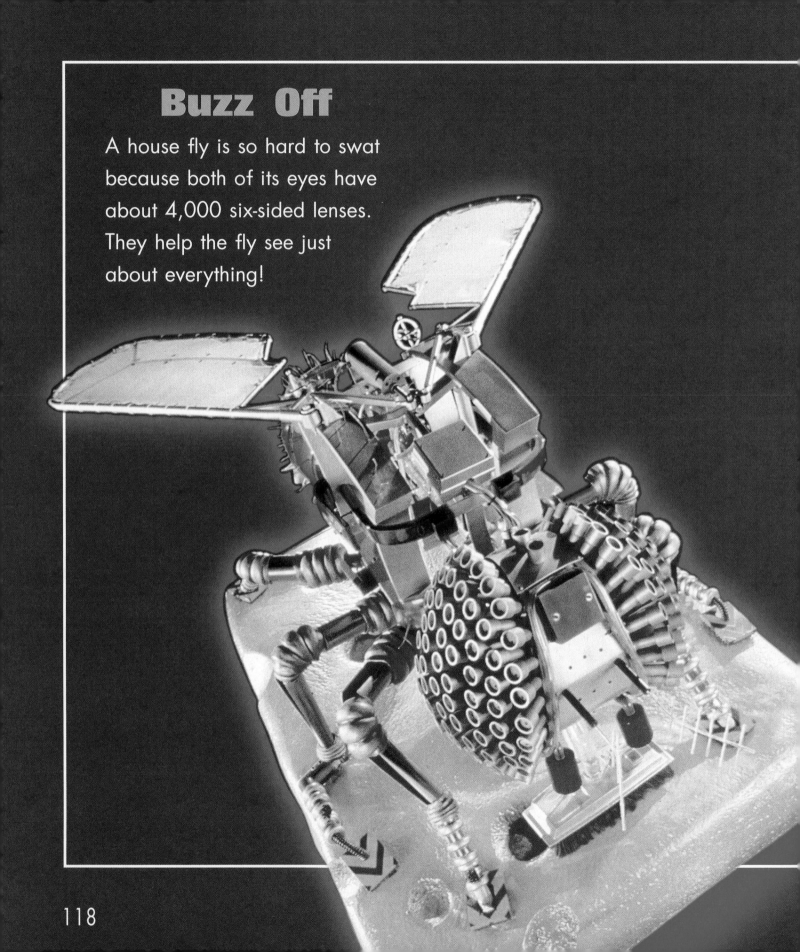

Take Off

Grasshoppers can hop and fly. So this robot has powerful springs in its two rear legs that work like the rear-leg muscles in a real grasshopper. Its muscles help it fly up, up, and away!

• **RESPONSE ACTIVITY** •

Ready Robot Puppets

If you had a robot, how would
your robot help you? Make a robot puppet
and act out all the ways it could help.

YOU WILL NEED:

- a cardboard tube or rolled-up paper • tape • glue
- collage materials • construction paper • markers

1 Use the tube for the robot's body. Draw a face on the tube.

2 Add arms and legs to the robot's body.

3 Decorate your robot. Think of things you would like your robot to do for you.

Use your puppet to show how a robot could help you.

The Absent-

by Javier Rondón   translated by Kathryn Corbett

The Absent-Minded Toad

Javier Rondón

Illustrated by Marcela Cabrera

KM Kane/Miller Book Publishers

Minded Toad

illustrated by Marcela Cabrera

123

A toad
of rainbow colors—
Orange, green,
and brown—

Made out a list
one morning
To take with him
to town.

Butter for tortillas,
Jam to put on toast.
He looked around his kitchen
For what he needed most.

A flower in his blue cap,
Around his leg a bell.
He smiled into his mirror.
He did look very well!

127

Then off he went to market—
Hop, hop, hop!
Looking in the windows
Of every kind of shop.

He stopped on the corner
Where the fruit seller sells
Fruits of many colors—
Oh, what lovely smells!

What a crowd of people
Dressed in their best!
Choosing cheese and brown eggs
Fresh from the nest.

131

"Tomatoes from my garden!"
The tomato seller said.
"Here, lady, try one—
Fresh and ripe and red!"

The toad hopped round the market
Almost all the day.
In all that crowd of people
He nearly lost his way.

At last he got home safely
And put his feet up.
He drank some warm milk
From his old blue cup.

135

He went for bread and butter
And then he said, "Oh, my!
I hopped all round the market,
But nothing did I buy!"

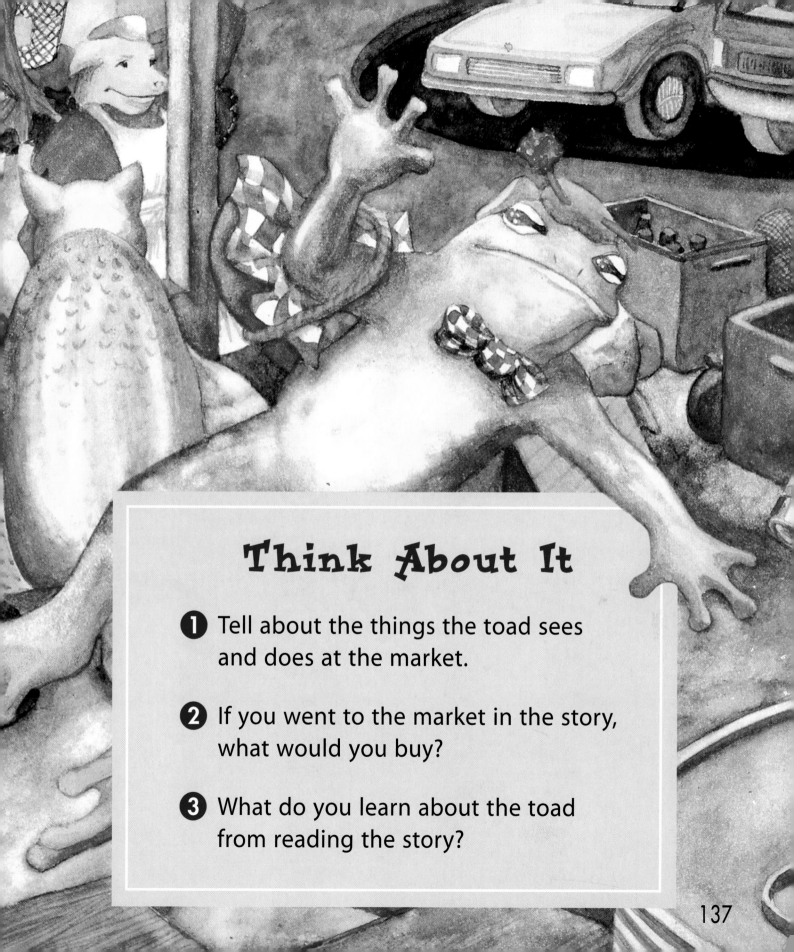

Think About It

❶ Tell about the things the toad sees and does at the market.

❷ If you went to the market in the story, what would you buy?

❸ What do you learn about the toad from reading the story?

137

Meet the Author
Javier Rondón

Javier Rondón grew up in Venezuela, in South America. His home was filled with art materials, and his two older sisters were very creative. He says that he is as absent-minded as the toad in this story, and often misplaces his keys and pencils.

Meet the Illustrator

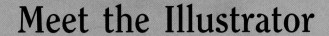

Marcela Cabrera

Marcela Cabrera is from Colombia, a country in South America. She went to art school in Venezuela and now makes her home there. *The Absent-Minded Toad* is the first children's book she illustrated.

Visit *The Learning Site!*
www.harcourtschool.com

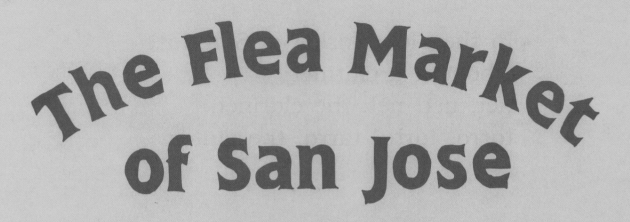

The Flea Market of San Jose

arranged and translated by José-Luis Orozco
illustrated by Elisa Kleven

In the Flea Market of San Jose
I bought a guitar,
tarra, tarra, tarra, the guitar.

CHORUS
You can go, you can go
to the Flea Market of San Jose.
You can go, you can go
to the Flea Market of San Jose.

In the Flea Market of San Jose
I bought a clarinet,
net, net, net, the clarinet,
tarra, tarra, tarra, the guitar.

You can go . . .

In the Flea Market of San Jose
I bought a violin,
lin, lin, the violin,
net, net, net, the clarinet,
tarra, tarra, tarra, the guitar.

You can go . . .

• Response Activity •

To Market

Act out a busy market scene with classmates!

Decide who will play these parts:
- the toad
- sellers in the market
- other shoppers

Think about what your character would say and do in the market.

Set up the classroom
like a market, and act
out the story.

If you like, act out the
story for family members
or other classes.

145

Tumbleweed Stew

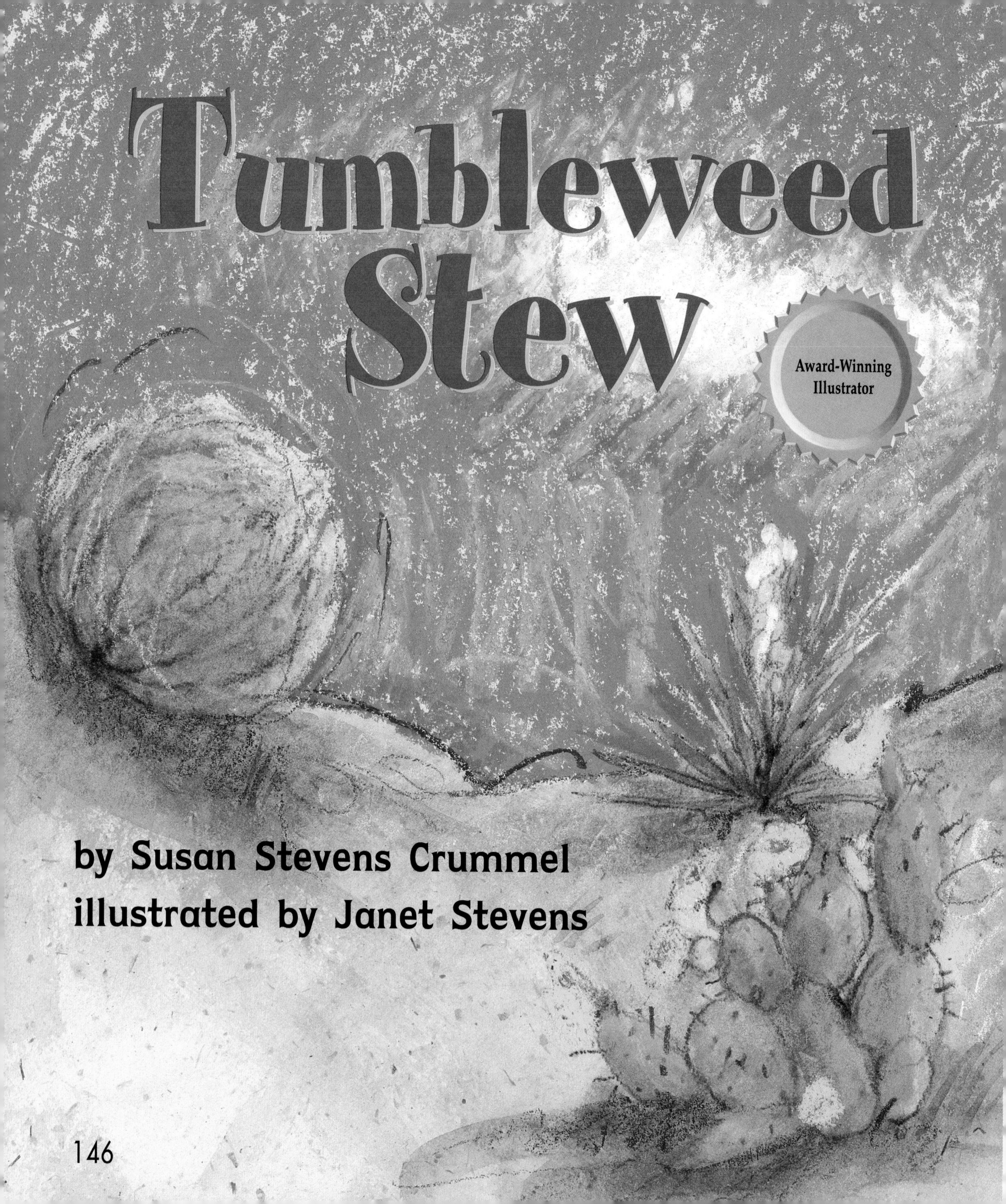

by Susan Stevens Crummel

illustrated by Janet Stevens

Award-Winning Illustrator

Jack Rabbit opened his eyes. He stretched and looked up at the pretty blue sky.

Jack's tummy growled. He thought,
"The sun is up. The sky is blue!
What a great day for tumbleweed stew!"
He hopped along, jumping over brush
and cactus.

Before long, he came to a big gate. Over the gate it said TWO-CIRCLE RANCH. Jack slipped under the fence and into a herd of cattle.

"Moo!" said Longhorn. "Move on!"
"Well, howdy," Jack said. "How do you do?
How would you like some tumbleweed stew?"

"There's no such thing as tumbleweed
stew," said Longhorn, munching the
dry grass.

"Not a nice place," thought Jack. He ran
down the path to the ranch house.
"Anyone home?" he called.
"NO!" he heard from inside. "Go away!"
"How about some lunch?" asked Jack.

Armadillo came out onto the porch. "This is my ranch," she said. "This is my food and you can't have any!"

Jack took a chance. He said,
"But I would like to cook for <u>you</u>.
Have you heard of tumbleweed stew?"
"There's no such thing as tumbleweed stew," Armadillo said.

Before Armadillo could blink, Jack started a fire. He spied an old pot and filled it with water. He set the pot of water on the fire. After a while, he stuffed a big tumbleweed into the pot.

Armadillo looked into the pot. Jack took
a taste and said,
"It smells so good. It tastes good, too.
But it needs more, this tumbleweed stew."
"Well," said Armadillo, "There might be
some carrots in my house."

Soon the tumbleweed

and carrots

were cooking in the
big pot.

Buzzard floated down to take a look. "I can smell this food way up in the sky! It needs onions," he said. "I'll fly home and get some."

Soon the tumbleweed,

carrots,

and onions
were cooking in the big pot.

Then Deer trotted over and looked into the pot. "This stew needs corn," he said. "I'll be right back."

Soon the tumbleweed, carrots,

onions,

and corn

were cooking in the big pot.

Skunk scampered up to the pot. "Smells good," she said. "But where are the potatoes? I'll go dig some up."

Soon the tumbleweed, carrots,

onions, corn,

and potatoes were
cooking in the big pot.

Rattlesnake slithered over with some celery.
"You can't make stew without celery," he said.

Soon, the tumbleweed, carrots,

onions, corn,
potatoes,

and celery

were cooking in the big pot.

163

Armadillo, Buzzard, Deer, Skunk, and
Rattlesnake gathered around the pot
of stew. They watched it bubble and steam.

At last Jack cried,
    "It took a while, but thanks to you,
    It's time to eat this tumbleweed stew!"
The animals ate and ate until every bite of
stew was gone.

Armadillo couldn't move. Buzzard couldn't
fly. Deer couldn't trot. Skunk couldn't
scamper. Rattlesnake couldn't slither.
They put their heads down and fell asleep.
Jack slept too, but not for long.

Jack Rabbit opened his eyes. He stretched and looked up at the pretty blue sky. His tummy growled. He thought,

"Another day for being sly—
What a great day for cactus pie!"

Think About It

1 How does Jack Rabbit get the other animals to put vegetables in the stew?

2 Would you want to have Jack Rabbit for a friend? Tell why or why not.

3 What did you learn about the characters from looking at the pictures? What else do the pictures tell you?

Susan

Meet the Author
and the Illustrator
Susan Stevens Crummel
and
Janet Stevens

"Tumbleweed Stew" takes place in Texas, where Susan Stevens Crummel and her sister Janet Stevens grew up. The sisters worked together on the story.

Susan wanted the characters in the story to be animals that live in Texas. Janet kept drawing them until she liked the way they looked. "The best part of making this story was working with my sister," said Janet.

Janet

Visit *The Learning Site!*
www.harcourtschool.com

169

Response Activity

Make a Tumble-Snack

Each animal in "Tumbleweed Stew" added something to the stew. You can make your own tumble-snack.

YOU WILL NEED:

pretzels

raisins

popcorn

nuts

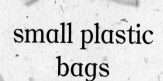
small plastic bags

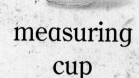
measuring cup

large self-closing plastic bags

3 cups popcorn

1 cup nuts

2 cups pretzels

2 cups raisins

- Measure each ingredient and pour into a large plastic bag.

- Close the bag. Take turns shaking the bag to "tumble" your snack.

- Pour or scoop out the snack into small bags.

Now eat your delicious Tumble-Snack!

LITTLE BEAR'S FRIEND

by ELSE HOLMELUND MINARIK

pictures by MAURICE SENDAK
by the author and artist of LITTLE BEAR

An I CAN READ Book®

Award-Winning Author and Illustrator

Little Bear and Emily

Little Bear sat in the top
of a high tree.
He looked all about him
at the wide, wide world.

He saw the green hills.

He saw the river.

And far, far away

he saw the blue sea.

He saw the tops of trees.

He saw his own house.

He saw Mother Bear.

He could hear the wind sing.

And he could feel the wind

on his fur, on his eyes,

on his little black nose.

He shut his eyes,

and let the wind brush him.

He opened his eyes,

and saw two little squirrels.

"Play with us," they said.

"No time," said Little Bear.

"I have to go home for lunch."

He began to climb down,
and saw four little birds.
"Look at us," they said,
"we can fly."

"I can, too," said Little Bear,
"but I always fly down.
I can't fly up
or sideways."

He climbed down some more,

and saw a little green worm.

"Hello," said the little green worm.

"Talk to me."

"Some other time," said Little Bear.

"I have to go home for lunch."

He climbed all the way down,

and there he saw a little girl.

"I think I am lost,"
said the little girl.

"Could you see the river
from the treetop?"

"Oh, yes," said Little Bear,

"I could see the river.

Do you live there?"

"Yes," said the little girl.

"My name is Emily.

And this is my doll Lucy."

"I am Little Bear, and
I can take you to the river.
What is in that basket?"

"Cookies," said Emily. "Have some."

"Thank you. I love cookies."

"So do I," said Emily.

They walked along eating cookies
and talking,
and soon they came to the river.

"I see our tent," said Emily,
"and my mother and father."

"And I hear my mother calling,"
said Little Bear.
"I have to go home for lunch.
Good-by, Emily."

"Good-by, Little Bear.

Come back and play with me."

"I will," said Little Bear.

Little Bear went skipping home.

He hugged Mother Bear and said,

"Do you know what I just did?"

"What did you just do, Little Bear?"

"I climbed to a treetop,
and I saw the wide world.
I climbed down again, and I saw
two squirrels, four little birds
and a little green worm.
Then I climbed all the way down,
and what do you think I saw?"

"What did you see?"

"I saw a little girl named Emily.
She was lost so I helped her
to get home.
And now I have a new friend.
Who do you think it is?"

"The little green worm,"
said Mother Bear.

Little Bear laughed.

"No," he said, "it is Emily.
Emily and I are friends."

Think About It

1 What is the most important thing Little Bear does in the story? What else does he do?

2 Would you like to have a friend like Little Bear? Tell why or why not.

3 How can you tell that Little Bear and Emily will be friends?

About the Author

Else Holmelund Minarik

Else Holmelund Minarik was four years old when she and her family left Denmark and moved to the United States. As a grown-up, she became a first-grade teacher. She began writing stories for children when she couldn't find good books for her first graders to read.

Else Holmelund Minarik wrote five books about Little Bear. The story you just read is from one of those books.

Meet the Illustrator

Maurice Sendak

Maurice Sendak grew up in Brooklyn, in New York City. He was the youngest of three children. He has strong memories of his childhood, which he uses in his writing and illustrating work. He is one of the most famous illustrators of books for children.

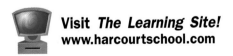
Visit *The Learning Site!*
www.harcourtschool.com

A Good Neighbor Skit

Little Bear is a good neighbor. He helped Emily when she was lost, and he made a new friend.

Work with a partner to create a skit that shows how to be a good neighbor.

1 Brainstorm a list of things that good neighbors do. Talk about times when someone was a good neighbor to you. What did the person do? How did you feel?

2 Decide what you will act out in your skit.

3 Write down your skit. Show one or more ways to be a good neighbor.

4 Perform your skit for your classmates.

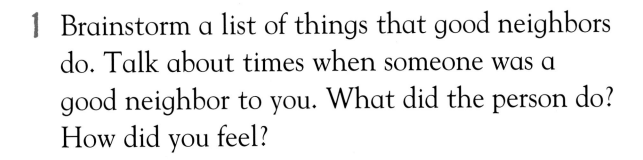

Glossary

What Is a Glossary?

A glossary is like a small dictionary. This glossary is here to help you. You can look up a word and then read a sentence that uses that word. Some words have a picture to help you.

al·most   The bag is **almost** full, but a few more apples will fit.

bears

bears   Some **bears** are brown, but polar bears are white.

be·fore   Turn out the lights **before** you go.

be·gan   We ran inside when it **began** to rain.

blue   I painted the sea **blue** in my picture.

buy   We **buy** things in stores.

blue

car·ry   I will **carry** this box outside.

chil·dren   There are twenty **children** in our class.

climb   A cat can **climb** a tree.

children

197

Earth

fire

full

col·ors　The sky changes **colors** at sunset.

cook　Dad will **cook** dinner tonight.

coun·try　Mexico is a **country** near the United States.

Earth　We live on the planet **Earth**.

fire　The **fire** in the fireplace made the room bright and warm.

food　We went out to buy **food** for lunch.

full　The glass is **full** of milk.

gone　Sara was here, but now she's **gone**.

great　Everyone had a **great** time at the party.

heads The children put their hats on their **heads.**

hear It is hard to **hear** people when they whisper.

heard I **heard** the teacher say it was time for reading.

laugh People **laugh** when funny things happen.

love I **love** my parents.

might I **might** ride my bike after school.

most I play soccer after school **most** days.

moved We **moved** the chairs into a circle.

laugh

moved

name

orange

name   My **name** is Mariana.

new   How do you like my **new** bike?

nice   We like to play outside when the weather is **nice.**

once   I have been to the zoo only **once.**

on·ly   If **only** we could eat pizza every day!

or·ange   I love to wear my **orange** shirt.

place   Put the book back in the same **place** you found it.

please   **Please** hand me a sheet of paper.

pret·ty   That butterfly is **pretty.**
Our team played **pretty** well today.

room   The kitchen is the **room** I like best in our house.

school   We go to **school** five days a week.

should   You **should** brush your teeth after you eat.

smiled   The girls **smiled** at each other.

sor·ry   Ana is **sorry** that she spilled the milk.

sound   The door made a loud **sound** when it slammed shut.

spe·cial   This ring is **special** because it was my grandmother's.

room

school

together

town

**United States
of America**

thought   I **thought** you would like that book!

to·geth·er   The four of us sat **together** at one table.

took   Jim **took** the book home.

town   A **town** may grow from just a few houses.

try   I'll **try** to reach the high shelf.

U·ni·ted States of A·mer·i·ca   People come from all over the world to live in the **United States of America.**

warm   A thick blanket keeps me **warm** in winter.

wa·ter　The **water** we drink once fell as rain.

while　We waited **while** Sam got dressed.

world　How long would it take for a plane to fly around the **world?**

write　I **write** my name on my drawings.

water

write

Acknowledgments

For permission to reprint copyrighted material, grateful acknowledgment is made to the following sources:

Candlewick Press, Cambridge, MA: Cover illustration from *Leon and Bob* by Simon James. Copyright © 1997 by Simon James.

Crown Publishers, Inc.: *Me on the Map* by Joan Sweeney, illustrated by Annette Cable. Text copyright © 1996 by Joan Sweeney; illustrations copyright © 1996 by Annette Cable.

Dutton Children's Books, a division of Penguin Putnam Inc.: From "The Flea Market of San Jose"/ "La Pulga de San José" in *Diez Deditos/Ten Little Fingers,* selected, arranged and translated by José-Luis Orozco, illustrated by Elisa Kleven. Lyrics and music arrangement copyright © 1997 by José-Luis Orozco; illustrations copyright © 1997 by Elisa Kleven.

Ediciones Ekaré, Caracas, Venezuela: The Absent-Minded Toad by Javier Rondón, illustrated by Marcela Cabrera. © 1988 by Ediciones Ekaré. Originally published in Spanish under the title *El Sapo Distraido.*

HarperCollins Publishers: "Little Bear and Emily" from *Little Bear's Friend* by Else Holmelund Minarik, illustrated by Maurice Sendak. Text copyright © 1960 by Else Holmelund Minarik; illustrations copyright © 1960 by Maurice Sendak.

Elizabeth M. Hauser: "Our Cat" from *Rhymes About Us* by Marchette Chute. Text copyright © 1974. Published by E. P. Dutton.

The Owl Group: "Visit the Robot Zoo" from *Chickadee* Magazine, Jan/Feb 1998. Text © 1998 by Bayard Press.

Philomel Books, a division of Penguin Putnam Inc.: Illustration by Ed Young from *Cats Are Cats,* compiled by Nancy Larrick. Illustration copyright © 1988 by Ed Young.

Simon & Schuster Books for Young Readers, Simon & Schuster Children's Publishing Division: Cover illustration from *Ask Mr. Bear* by Marjorie Flack. Copyright © 1932 by Macmillan Publishing Company; copyright renewed 1960 by Hilma H. Barnum. Cover illustration by Pam Paparone from *Fire Fighters* by Norma Simon. Illustration copyright © 1995 by Pam Paparone.

Photo Credits

Michael Campos Photography, 31, 55, 75, 96, 97; BBH exhibits, Inc., 116-119; Michael Campos Photography, 120-121; courtesy Ediciones Ekaré, 138-139; Michael Campos Photography, 145, 170, 171; Bradford Bachrach, 192; Allan Tannenbaum/Sygma, 193
All other photos by Harcourt:
Tom Sobolik/Black Star; Walt Chyrnwski/Black Star; Todd Bigelow/Black Star; George Robinson/Black Star; Mark Perlstein/Black Star; Brian Payne/Black Star; Larry Evans/Black Star; Ken Hayden/Black Star; Dale Higgins/Black Star

Illustration Credits

Keith Baker, Cover Art; Brenda York, 4-9; Holly Keller, 10-27, 30-31; Ed Young, 28-29; Tracy Sabin, 31, 54, 96-97; Annette Cable, 32-53; George Kreif, 55; Betsy Everitt, 56-75; Jose Aruego and Ariane Dewey, 76-95; Dagmar Fehlau, 98-115; Marcela Cabrera, 122-139, 144-145; Elisa Kleven, 140-143; Janet Stevens, 146-171; Maurice Sendak, 172-195